KU-187-300

Easy Peasy

AWESOME PAWSOME

DOG TRAINING
FOR
KiDS

Easy Peasy AWESOME PAWSOME DOG TRAINING FOR KIDS

Steve Mann

BLINK
bringing you closer

First published in the UK by Blink Publishing
An imprint of Bonnier Books UK
The Plaza, 535 Kings Road, London SW10 0SZ
Owned by Bonnier Books
Sveavägen 56, Stockholm, Sweden

facebook.com/blinkpublishing
twitter.com/blinkpublishing

Trade Paperback – 978-1-788704-45-8
Ebook – 978-1-788704-46-5

All rights reserved. No part of the publication may be reproduced, stored in a retrieval system, transmitted or circulated in any form or by any means, electronic, mechanical, photocopying, recording or otherwise, without prior permission in writing of the publisher.

A CIP catalogue of this book is available from the British Library.

Designed by Perfect Bound Ltd
Printed and bound in Poland

1 3 5 7 9 10 8 6 4 2

Illustration copyright © Adam Hayes, 2021
Copyright © Steve Mann and Martin Roach, 2021

Steve Mann and Martin Roach have asserted their moral right to be identified as the authors of this work in accordance with the Copyright, Designs and Patents Act 1988.

Every reasonable effort has been made to trace copyright holders of material reproduced in this book, but if any have been inadvertently overlooked the publishers would be glad to hear from them.

This book is not intended to be a substitute for veterinary advice.
If you are concerned that your dog has a behavioural or other disorder, you should seek veterinary advice. The author and publisher will not be liable for any loss or damage in connection with or arising out of the performance or use of methods described and contained in this book.

Blink Publishing is an imprint of Bonnier Books UK
www.bonnierbooks.co.uk

This book is dedicated to
everyone that chooses to be
kind to all animals

About Steve

Steve Mann is a bit of a clever clogs when it comes to dog training.

Like you, Steve fell in love with dogs at a young age and since then has worked all of his life to help educate people and dogs to live a happy, peaceful and fun life together.

As well as writing books such as this **CLASSIC**, Steve's other job is teaching people all over the world how to be professional dog trainers, so he can reach as many owners and dogs as possible to help and support them through all of their dog training adventures.

Contents

First things first

let's talk about your dog

The best exercises to teach your dog

IF YOU'RE GOOD ENOUGH...

YOU'RE OLD ENOUGH.

FIRST THINGS FIRST

Every epic journey starts with a single step, so let's make sure we take the most important steps first.

We're going to learn how to become your dog's favourite teacher, then we're going to look at dog training kit, safety, then move on to the training of our two classic exercises, Sit and Down.

Right, eyes to the front, sit up straight, and let's get learning!

WELCOME TO THE WORLD OF AWESOME PAWSOME TRAINING!

Hello!

I'm Steve.

I've always been obsessed with dogs.

Not just *interested* or *keen to find out more* . . .

OBSESSED!

Strangely enough, I wasn't as lucky as you growing up because my family never had a dog, which I think only increased my obsession with our furry friends.

There used to be a few neighbours' dogs that I would play with all day out in the streets. I used to spend my long summer school holidays in Ireland, and my family over there always had dogs knocking around on their farms for me to hang out with.

One day – and I can't tell you what a big deal this was for me – a local dog training school opened up near where I lived!

My excitement level when I heard this news was the same as if a rocket ship had landed in the middle of the playground, or as if I had been offered free ice cream for life.

I didn't let the mere fact that I didn't own a dog get in the way!

I was DEFINITELY going to attend!

So, first week, there I was, a kid without a dog, surrounded by adults WITH a dog, waiting to go into class.

I was really shy when I was younger. I couldn't even look adults in the eye when they spoke to me and the best I could ever reply was 'yes', 'no' or maybe a shrug of the shoulders.

However, chatting to dogs? Now that was easy!

Waiting by the entrance to the dog training classes, the adults stood talking to each other, ignoring the dogs. There I was, crouched down on the floor, talking to the dogs, ignoring the adults.

All of a sudden, the doors to the hall were thrown open and, with wide eyes, I saw the technicoloured world that I wanted to stay in for the rest of my life. The world of dog training.

If I close my eyes now, I can still see the bright colours of the striped dog jumps, hear the tippy-tap of the dogs' feet on the hall floor, the sound of their breathing and the buzz of the excited praise coming from the owners. I can still recall the sensation of petting the dogs, their hair running between my fingers, and I can still smell the dog treats, along with the sweet aroma of cleaning fluids should any of the dogs have had an 'accident'!

Everything seemed bigger, louder, clearer and better.

THAT'S how I felt when I stepped through the doors of my first dog training class – I instantly KNEW this was where I wanted to be for the rest of my life.

The magical world of dog training.

WELCOME!

COME ON IN....

MY FIRST COMPETITION

Even at my ripe old age, I recall the very first competition I entered with a dog.

Remember, I didn't even have a dog of my own at the time.

No, the dog I rocked up with to the competition was Flo, a pretty big Rottweiler. In fact, scratch that. Rewind. She wasn't 'pretty big'. She was very pretty and she was VERY BIG. In fact, she was MASSIVE.

And there's me, a skinny little ten-year-old on the other end of the lead. Like a monkey holding a rhino.

Flo was owned by the man who lived three doors down from my house. Me and the other kids used to play out in the dead-end street where we lived, and Flo would be out all day with us. She only went back indoors for the same reason we did when the sun started going down – because we were all hungry! Flo didn't even have to go home for a wee. In fact, come to think of it, ahem . . . neither did I!

I knew the Dog Obedience Competition at the local fair was coming up because I'd seen a leaflet on the noticeboard of the local youth club that I used to go to.

I had three weeks to practise for the competition, which included:

 'Heel Work' (I had to look that up, but it's basically strolling around a course with your dog walking nicely next to you, off-lead)

 a 'Retrieve' (the dog had to fetch something you'd thrown and bring it back to you, then sit in front of you with it in their mouth until the judge told you to take it)

 a 'Down Stay' (asking your dog to lie down, in a row, next to all of the other dogs as you walk ten metres away, for one minute).

Man, did Flo and I train hard for those three weeks!

The competition was in the school summer holidays and while most of my friends were knocking on the doors of their other friends to go out to play, I was knocking on Flo's door, grabbing her favourite toy and a bag full of treats and heading over to the park to play. I mean train. Not really, I mean PLAY.

REMEMBER:
ALL TRAINING SHOULD FEEL LIKE PLAY, ESPECIALLY FOR THE DOG.

I had the BEST time and I wanted to really do Flo proud at the competition.

We got really good at our Heel Work, Retrieves and Stays at the park, even with the distraction of my friends trying to put us off by kicking the football near us . . . over and OVER again! Good! I wanted to train with distractions. I knew there would be plenty of distractions at the competition field, what with ice-cream vans, bouncy castles and people staring at us, as me and Flo tried our best.

I knew it was great to practise with distractions, to try and mimic what would actually be happening on the day. But what about WHERE it was going to happen?

I had heard owners at class moaning to the trainer that their 'silly dog always does the exercises perfectly at class, but never does them properly at the park'.

'That's because you only practise at class, not at the park, so you're the silly one,' I would say (VERY quietly under my breath).

BINGO! That was it!

If I wanted Flo to feel comfortable and happy when doing the exercises at the competition field, we needed to practise in that exact same location! So that's what we did; me and Flo would walk the extra couple of miles each day and crawl under the fence at the school playing fields where the competition was going to be held, sometimes having to hide behind the bins together if we heard the caretaker coming!

We practised in the exact location where the competition would take place, so Flo could get used to the sights, sounds and most importantly the SMELLS of that field. We went there every day so for Flo it just became a home from home.

I say we practised every day, but don't think we just did Heel Work, Retrieves and Stays all the time. Not even I could bear that! I thought back then – and I still do now – that if your dog has fun and wants to hang around with you, then everything else is going to be pretty

EASY PEASY.

I figured that if we were only ever a few moments from a fun game with her *favourite* toy, a game of 'catch' (and eat!) with her *favourite* treats or seconds away from her *favourite* belly rubs, then why would she dream of running away from me at the Heel Work, or not bring the Retrieve toy back to me for a game, or not wait for me to return on the Stays?

That was my plan anyway!

So the majority of our time was spent just hanging, playing and enjoying each other's company. Don't knock it – that's my full-time job now!

All was going great . . .

But then the night before the competition came around.

Even writing this, forty years later, I'm getting a horrible knot in my tummy and my legs feel hollow.

As I lay wide awake in bed, I felt sick.

I got so nervous.

This was a competition for adults, not kids.

Even in normal times, I still couldn't look an adult in the eye. Tomorrow, I was planning on going out and competing against them.

Tomorrow, I'll be honest, I was planning on **beating** them.

The Big Day

Flo and I walked to the competition at the school playing fields – the same, now-familiar route we had taken each morning during all of those previous weeks. This felt different, though. There were hundreds of people there and an excited buzz of chatting and laughing. I could hear bells going off on the 'Test Your Strength' machine and cheers erupting when someone managed to knock a coconut to the ground at the shy.

Flo was AWESOME, even before we started the competition. Every time there was a loud cheer or another strange noise, I'd pull out the toy to play with her or drop her a piece of cheese.

Pretty soon, any distracting noise became the signal for me and Flo to look at each other! I loved that dog.

I registered myself and Flo to enter the competition and I was given a number to pin on my chest, which was so large that I had to tuck most of it into my shorts!

We were due to go into the roped-off arena in ten minutes.

I began to feel sick with nerves again. I remember sitting on the grass with Flo, rubbing her belly to try and relax. I stroked her ear as she put her head in my lap and I realised something that has stuck with me forever.

Flo didn't care.

Flo didn't know it was a competition.

She wasn't nervous.

She didn't care what other people thought.

She just wanted to have a good time playing with me.

Basically, she was wise enough to know that she couldn't eat a rosette!

Who cares!

That was one of the most important lessons I've ever learned from a dog – and, believe me, I learn from dogs every single day of my life.

THE MOST IMPORTANT THING FOR YOU AND YOUR DOG IS TO HAVE FUN TOGETHER!

I puffed up my chest, told Flo I loved her and the pair of us marched into the centre of the ring, where I had to shake hands with the judge before starting.

As we walked, the people watching were grinning. Were they smiling because they thought, *Who's this silly little ten-year-old with the massive dog?* Or, even worse, were they grinning because they thought I was *cute*?

Before we started our Heel Work, my heart was thumping out of my mouth; I remember stroking Flo one last time but, to be honest, I was just trying to wipe the sweat from my clammy hands!

One last, long breath, then I looked at Flo, she looked at me and in we went . . .

Well, I can hardly describe what happened next.

It happens to me all the time now when I'm in 'the zone' with my dog.

We just tune in.

It's like we're looking at each other through a Smarties tube and don't register any other distractions.

I don't remember seeing anything else other than Flo.

I don't remember any sounds other than the judge telling me to 'Turn left, turn right, about turn.' (I didn't really know what 'about turn' meant but I guessed right!) For Retrieves, I know he said, 'throw the dumbbell', 'send the dog', 'take the object'. And finally, for the Stays, I recall the judge shouting like a sergeant major in the army . . .

LEEEEEAVE THE DOG!

It was over.

It felt like seconds but all of those days and weeks of practice paid off because . . .

WE WON!

At the end of the day, Flo and I had to go up to get our trophy and rosette.

I still have that trophy to this day, but not as a reminder of the *competition*.

As a reminder of the *training*.

You see, my friends thought I was crazy to do weeks and weeks of training just for a few minutes' pleasure at a competition and to win a silly rosette.

They didn't understand.

The pleasure wasn't in the few minutes' competition; the pleasure was in the weeks and weeks of training.

The rosette WAS silly, though – I swapped it for three tennis balls so Flo and I could go play some more!

THE SECRET TO BECOMING YOUR DOG'S FAVOURITE TEACHER!

What do you prefer: *playing* or *learning*? (Be honest!)

How cool a teacher would you be if your pupils couldn't tell the difference between a lesson and a game?

That's how cool a teacher **you're** going to be!

I want you to teach your dog the way YOU'D love to be taught, with two Golden Rules for both of you:

1. NO PRESSURE – EVER!

2. ALWAYS FUN!

Dogs learn the same way you and I do.

If we behave in a certain way and, as a result, we receive something nice in exchange, too right we're going to want to repeat that behaviour again!

and again!
and again!
and again!
and again!
and again!
and again!
and again!
and again!
and again!

Sadly, some unlucky people have to do certain things because if they don't, they get something nasty, such as a telling off or punishment. However, that definitely doesn't follow our two golden rules and DEFINITELY isn't the way we're ever going to interact with our dogs. It's just not the **EASY PEASY** way!

In addition, if we're mean to our dogs, they're not going to enjoy being with us – and what's the point of that?!

Only a twit would ever be nasty to a dog.

Right, back on track.

Swapping nice things that your dog loves for the nice behaviours they do for you in return is called Positive Reinforcement by fancy dog trainers – this basically means giving your dog a reward for a job well done.

Don't worry, I'm not going to dwell on boring and confusing long words, that would be

phenomenally discombobulating (!)

– let's just agree that when we give our dogs nice rewards for the cool behaviours they do, then everyone's happy!

'That's all well and good,' I hear you say (you're very well-spoken for a kid, aren't you!?), 'but what about when my dog does a naughty behaviour?'

FOR A DOG, THERE'S NO SUCH THING AS 'GOOD' _OR_ 'NAUGHTY' BEHAVIOURS —

ONLY BEHAVIOURS.

I've got an answer for that, too!

Dogs do things so that they can earn a reward.

However, the **AWESOME PAWSOME DOG TRAINER** (YOU!) knows that if we don't want our dog to do any unwanted behaviour, such as jump up at visitors or pull on their lead, we need to teach them what to do INSTEAD.

We need to reward our dog for doing a nicer behaviour.

Let me give you an example . . .

Let's say your dog has a habit of pulling on the lead when they see another doggy pal and they want to go over to say 'Howdy doody'.

Now, when your dog pulls on the lead, if you mistakenly *reward* that behaviour by running over to let the dogs say, 'Hello', then guess what your dog's going to do the NEXT time they see another dog? You guessed it, they'll pull on the lead again!

DISASTER!

In this example, a nicer behaviour than pulling on the lead would be for you to wait until your dog looks to YOU and ONLY THEN do you say, 'Go on then, say hello!' and the pair of you jog over for your canine meet-and-greet.

Your dog looking to you is a nicer behaviour because they can't look at you AND pull on the lead at the same time.

Here's another example: how about if your dog jumps up at visitors to say, 'Hello'?

Simples!

Teach your dog that people only say, 'Hello' to them when their bum is on the ground (your dog's bum, not the visitor's. That'd be weird. Funny, but weird).

In this example, sitting is a fab behaviour for your dog to do instead of jumping up because, unless they're some sort of magical hover hound, they can't sit *and* jump at the same time.

With lots of fun practice, what behaviour do you think your dog is going to be super-keen to do the next time they want a visitor to say, 'Hello' to them?

You've guessed it: SIT!

So here's the plan: to stop your dog doing an unwanted behaviour in the future, teach them what you want them to do INSTEAD. Not forgetting to give them plenty of rewards when they get it right!

What kind of teacher would YOU prefer to be taught by? One that tells you off for standing in class or one that gives you sweets for sitting on your chair in class?

I know which one I'd prefer!

THE KIT

As I said, I never had a dog when I was your age, so I used to mow lawns, wash cars AND do a paper round just so I could buy treats and toys for OTHER PEOPLE'S DOGS!

Now that I'm all grown up and get to live with five awesome dogs I get to buy stuff for them all the time!

It's important that we buy the RIGHT stuff, though, for several reasons, including safety, comfort and value for money. For example, it's no good buying your dog a toy that LOOKS good but gets destroyed into a thousand pieces only five seconds after you've given it to them!

Let's have a look at a few essentials that you'll need for your dog and, if you haven't got them yet, put them on your, or your dog's, birthday and Christmas wish list!

Lead

A good lead can be a life saver. Make sure it's comfortable to hold, is made from a nice, strong material and that the clip works reliably. I like a lead that is approximately two metres long so I can shorten it if I need to but if my dog is walking nicely next to me, the lead can be relaxed, making a 'smiling' shape.

Harness

This is so much more comfortable than a collar if your dog happens to pull on the lead. Make sure the harness fits nice and comfortably – you NEVER want your dog to be hurt.

Collar

NOW is the time that shopping gets fun! There's a huge range of funky collars to choose from. Make sure it fits nicely – not *too* loose but you should be able to comfortably slip two fingers between your dog's neck and the collar. That way you know it's not too tight.

Long Line

A long line is a five-to-ten metre lead which you attach to your dog's harness. This can be really handy when you're practising Recalls (see page 86) or when you're happy for your dog to roam around a little further from you, but it's not quite safe enough where you are for your dog to be completely off-lead. Always think: *safety first!*

Treats

Treats should always be tasty (let your dog be the judge!) and ideally nice and small so that your dog really appreciates them but doesn't get a full tummy too quickly. I like treats that are easy to handle, such as pieces of chicken, cubes of cheese or slices of frankfurter.

Spend an afternoon with your dog to discover what is their favourite treat. This will definitely be your dog's favourite afternoon, EVER!

Prepare ten different options and compare how happy your dog is when you deliver each one.

Let your dog sniff the treat though your fingers before they get to eat it.

What treat blasts your dog's happy-tail-o-meter off the scale?!

The most important thing about dog treats is that your dog LOVES them! In the same way that you will like certain foods that some of your friends don't, dogs also have personal preferences, so don't be afraid to try a few different ones to find out your dog's favourite.

26

WARNING

Some foods, such as chocolate and grapes, are poisonous for dogs!

Treat Pouch

Now, I know your dog INSISTS that you always have this when you're training and out on walks together! Your dog told me to make sure it's plenty BIG enough so you can load it with tons of tasty treats. Get one that clips onto your waistband or, even better, one that you can thread your belt through. That way, the weight of all of those treats won't make your jeans fall down to around your ankles! (I know someone that this happened to once, ahem!)

Poo Bags

Being an Awesome Pawsome Dog Trainer means being full of fun but it also means being responsible, or lucky. If you're *responsible*, make sure you bag up your dog's poop and throw it in the correct bin. If you're *lucky*, get your mum or dad to do it! It's a dirty job but everyone's gotta do it! Make sure the bags are strong. There's nothing worse than a surprise warm finger!

Toys

I always tell the owners who come to my dog training classes that the power of a toy isn't what it IS but what it DOES.

How does your dog like to play? Tug? Chase?

Whatever toys you choose, make sure you can both enjoy the game by playing together.

AWESOME PAWSOME TIP: IF YOU CAN, HAVE TWO TOYS EXACTLY THE SAME. WHEN YOU'RE PLAYING, IF YOUR DOG DOESN'T DROP TOY #1, QUICKLY PULL OUT TOY #2 AND START PLAYING WITH IT YOURSELF. YOUR DOG WILL SOON DROP TOY #1 WHEN THEY SEE HOW MUCH FUN YOU'RE HAVING WITH TOY #2!

Chews

Dogs love to chew. It's good for their teeth and helps them relax.

When your dog chews, a lot of feel-good emotions are released – a little like when you eat ice cream!

Chews come in lots of different textures, and your dog may prefer a softer chew one day and a tougher chew the next. Make sure you give your dog lots of opportunities for chewin' and chillin'. Have lots of chews available for your dog. It's so much better than your furry friend chewing your homework! (Or is it?!)

Bed

After a full day of playing and adventures, I love watching my dogs snuggling down for the night in their beds. Make sure your dog's bed is not too big, because they will want to curl up and feel secure, but also make sure it's not so small that all their legs dangle over the edge! Every now and then, have the bed washed to stop any creepy-crawlies interfering with your dog's peaceful dreams (and to stop it ponging out the house!).

SAFETY **FIRST**

Dogs are THE BEST but, like with all of the precious things in life, we need to be careful.

When I used to go into a posh shop with my mum, she made me put my hands in my pockets because I was always clumsily knocking expensive things off the shelves! The good news is, I'm not going to make you keep your hands in your pockets when you're with your dog, but we ARE going to have a few simple rules to keep everyone

HAPPY and SAFE.

Rule #1 — Never Approach An Unknown Dog Without The Owner's Or Your Parent's Permission.

I know it's tempting but the dog may be scared, injured or just not comfortable with people. When I was a child, I made a BIG mistake and ended up in hospital after I foolishly tried to cuddle an unknown dog. It wasn't the dog's fault; it was mine. Learn from my mistake!

Rule #2 — Play Nicely

Never lean on the dog when you're playing and always use a similar amount of strength as they are using with you. When I play tuggy with my Staffordshire bull terrier, who is called Pablo, I can be a little stronger than when I play with Nancy, my Chihuahua. (Although in Nancy's mind, she's the strongest dog in the world!)

Rule #3 | Don't Let Play Get Too Hyper

Sometimes dogs can get sooooo excited with games that they can become a little too wound up. Playing is great but don't allow your dog to become too hyper. Warning signs are high-pitched barking, staring eyes or their body becoming stiff. When hyper, the fun begins to stop, so I want to rely on you, as an Awesome Pawsome Trainer, to spot these warning signs and do something to make your dog more comfortable and relaxed. For example, I'd like you to pop the toys away and just scatter a few treats for your dog to sniff out and enjoy. Sniffing helps your dog to relax and maybe when they're ready, you can give them a chew to enjoy and chill out with.

CHEWS

Rule #4 | Know When To Stay Away

Awesome Pawsome Trainers don't go near any dog when they're eating or sleeping. They don't go near them if the dog is injured or sick and they certainly don't go after them if the dog is trying to move away.

The last thing we want is for the dog to worry that we're going to take away their food. How would you feel if someone reached over your shoulder and stole a chip from you the next time you're at McDonald's? Not very happy, I'm guessing!

If the dog is injured or sick, they won't want to upset *you* but they may be defensive and feel the need to growl or bite to tell you to go away, as they may mistakenly think the pain is connected to you, or they may worry that you'll make the pain worse. We never want to put that pressure on a dog.

Rule #5 — **Ask Permission**

If you don't ask, you don't get.

With Rule #1, I suggested that you always get permission from the dog's owner or your parent before interacting with an unknown dog – if you want to be even smarter than that, get permission from the dog as well!

Rather than you going over to the dog, instead crouch down, put your hand out and – if they're comfortable – the dog will come TO YOU and offer their 'sweet spot', the area on their body that they'd most like to be rubbed.

Now, as far as I'm concerned, if the dog doesn't come to you, that's double points! It tells me that you've read the situation really well: you gave the dog the choice whether to come to you or not and you were mature enough to accept that the petting was just too much for the dog to handle at that moment.

Well done you for being so considerate to the dog. THANK YOU!

Rule #6 — **Have Fun!**

If you, the adults who are there and the dog are all comfortable with the situation, THEN GO FOR IT!

TOP TIPS FOR AWESOME PAWSOME TRAINERS

Tip #1 Look After Your Tools

FIRST UP, BOTH YOU AND YOUR DOG CAN ONLY DO ANYTHING TO THE BEST OF YOUR ABILITY IF YOU LOOK AFTER YOUR TWO MOST IMPORTANT TOOLS: YOUR BRAIN AND YOUR BODY.

That means that you and your dog must always **eat** well, **sleep** well and **exercise** well. If any of those three targets aren't met, you simply can't be as good as you must be, to be part of Team **Awesome Pawsome!**

Tip #2 Look At The World From Your Dog's Point Of View

One of the most valuable skills an **Awesome Pawsome** Dog Trainer can have is the ability to look at the world from the dog's point of view. Think about how they experience life, living in our strange human world. Think about how they feel about training. This skill really helps you make decisions about when to step in to make them feel safe, proud, excited, happy, loved and determined to try their best.

Tip #3 Tomorrow's Another Day

Dog training is always an ongoing process, it's never a one-off event.

It's much better to take lots of tiny but fun steps in the right direction to achieve your goals, rather than putting too much pressure on you both. If it all goes wrong, don't worry – having fun is the most important thing!

Tip #4 Every Day's A School Day (Sorry!)

Awesome Pawsome Trainers know that every time they're with their dog, their dog is learning!

SO MAKE SURE
YOU REWARD
THE BEHAVIOURS
YOU WANT
MORE OF!

Tip #5 How Your Dog Feels Is Far More Important Than What They Do

This is where your body language expertise (see page 63) will be so valuable. If your dog is happy and feels safe, they'll confidently do what you ask them to – as long as you pay well!

Tip #6 Train With A Smile

Being an **Awesome Pawsome** Trainer is the best job in the world!

When you show the world that you're happy, your dog is likely to share in that joy also. Us humans and our dogs always learn best when we feel

Tip #7 Ask: 'How Can I Make This Easier For My Dog?'

Everyone wants to be successful, especially your dog!

Could you make training easier for them by changing the place you train, maybe changing the way you ask for behaviours or practising more?

There's no such thing as 'failure' for an **Awesome Pawsome** Trainer, only 'information'. If you ask your dog to do something and they don't do it, don't despair. Maybe ask for a two-second Sit rather than five seconds? Maybe practise your Recall in a less distracting location? Maybe don't ask for a Down when the ground is cold and icy?!

Silly dog trainers keep trying the same training even when it's not working, and expect a different result.

Great dog trainers make awesome changes to their training and get awesome results!

What are you waiting for?

LET'S GET TRAINING with a couple of classics: **Sit** and **Down**...

SIT

Ever wondered why teaching your dog to Sit is so important?

Well, it makes many, many other things soooooo much easier, such as popping the lead onto your wiggly and excited dog before a walk, teaching them not to jump up onto people to say hi, or for safety reasons at the park or roadside.

And it's so much nicer to ask your dog to Sit, rather than grabbing onto a nearby lamp post the second they see another dog on the other side of the road!

OK, tuck your shirt in, and let's get to work teaching your dog to SIT!

Have plenty of small tasty treats in your treat pouch and call your dog to you (to be honest, if your treats are super-tasty, chances are you probably won't have to call your dog to you, they'll be ready and waiting!).

1) Take a treat in your hand and hold it to your dog's nose.

2) When your dog sniffs the treat in your hand, slowly raise that hand over and above your dog's head. As your dog's head slowly follows the treat, you'll notice how their butt lowers towards the floor.

3) As soon as your dog's butt touches the floor, say, 'Good!' and allow your dog to take the treat from your hand.

4) Wipe the dog slobber from your hand onto your mum's dress and then have a another go!

Over the next five attempts, try to add a little longer between the time of your dog popping their butt onto the floor and you saying 'Good!' before giving them the treat for a job well done. The reason we are doing this is so that your dog learns to sit happily for longer periods of time.

Over the next five days, see if you can build up to a five-second Sit before treating!

Once you can get to a reliable five-second Sit before treating, I want you to do the same movement with your arm but DON'T have the treat in your hand.

Lure your dog's head up and over with your hand signal – to 'lure' is to use a treat to tempt your dog to move into the position you want them to be in. When their bottom kisses the floor (don't imagine that too much, it's odd!), say, 'Good!', hand your dog a treat FROM YOUR TREAT POUCH and then give your dog lots of praise and fuss for being so Pawsome!

The final step (which goes on forever until you're as old as me!) is to practise in as many different situations as possible:

 **On the lead**

 **Off the lead**

 **In the garden**

At the park

🐾 **Indoors**

🐾 **In the middle of play sessions**

🐾 **Before you go to school**

🐾 **Instead of doing the washing up (if you're lucky!)**

REMEMBER,

PRACTICE MAKES PERMANENT-

SO PRACTISE WELL AND PRACTISE OFTEN !

DOWN

The Down position is when your dog lies flat on the ground with their chest touching the ground.

I wonder how many situations we can think of where it would be handy to ask our dog to do a Down for us?

I'll go first:

🐾 **If we want to chill out on the floor watching telly AND give our dog a cuddle at the same time.**

🐾 **If we want our dog to stop wriggling as we brush their coat.**

🐾 **If we want to relax after a nice long walk with our dog and have an ice cream on a park bench.**

🐾 **If we want our dog to cool off under the shade of a tree on a warm summer's day.**

🐾 **If we meet a friend at the park who is a little unsure about dogs and we want to demonstrate there's nothing for your pal to be afraid of.**

Can you think of any other examples?

Teaching your dog to do a Down requires one VERY important skill that only Awesome Pawsome Trainers possess . . .

P A T I E N C E

To teach a Down successfully AND kindly, I want you to take teeny weeny, tiny, little bite-sized steps, so we can lay a really strong foundation and not put any pressure on your dog. Ready? Let's go!

1) With your dog's favourite treats in your pouch, ask them to Sit in front of you.

2) Take a treat in your hand and, with your dog remaining in the Sit position, place it under your dog's nose, by their chest, and slowly lure your dog's head towards the floor . . . but remember, I want their butt 'glued' to the floor. Here's where the patience comes in!

3) Don't expect to lure your dog all the way into a Down position on the first attempt – it's not a race! I want you to do ten successful repetitions of just luring your dog's head lower than their shoulder height and, when they do so, say, 'Good!' and give them a tasty treat each time.

After ten successful attempts, that's probably enough for your first session. Remember, you're asking your dog to bend and use muscles in ways they may not be used to – we don't want them to get sore from over-use.

WE ALWAYS WANT OUR AWESOME PAWSOME DOG TRAINING SESSIONS TO BE COMFORTABLE AND FUN.

Think about it: doing a quiz for a few minutes at school with five questions may be fun. But doing a quiz for hours and hours at school with 5,000 questions would be a

NIGHTMARE!

For your next Down training session, maybe tomorrow, I want you to use the treat to lower your dog's nose almost to the floor but – and here's the tricky part – because you are luring your dog's head even lower, they may be tempted to lift their butt up from the floor. That's only natural because, as they bend, their spine acts like a see-saw: one end goes down, so the other end lifts up. If you hold a pencil in front of you and then tip the point down, you'll see how the other end raises up. Same with your dog.

Except your dog (hopefully) doesn't have a rubber on their bum!

If your dog does get up out of their Sit position, no bother at all. That's just the dog training gods telling us that we've gone too far, too soon. Simply try again but don't lure your dog's head so low next time. It's important that we keep getting *success*, rather than trying the same thing over and over again but never succeeding. Who would ever want to play that game?!

When you can successfully lure (and then treat!) your dog for lowering their nose to the floor and keeping their butt on their floor at the same time, you're ready to go for the full Down . . .

4) With your dog sat in front of you, take a treat in your hand and lure their head towards the floor. As their nose approaches the floor, have a peek behind them and *as long as their butt remains grounded*, slowly slide the treat along the floor from between their two feet towards you.

What we want to see here is your dog remaining in a Sit, their head low and following the treat along the floor. As long as your dog is motivated to earn the tasty treat, they'll flatten out completely and drop into a Down position!

As soon as they do, say, 'Good!', give them the treat from your hand and AS LONG AS THEY REMAIN IN THE DOWN POSITION, keep slowly feeding them a series of individual treats. I want you to use the treats to illustrate to your dog that being in a Down PAYS REALLY WELL! If they get out of the Down position, no biggy at all, just stop feeding the treats.

Over several sessions, once you're confident that your dog will go Down smoothly as soon as you start luring, then you can begin to say 'Down' as you begin the lure.

When your dog is comfortably lying down when you ask them to, you can then continue to use your hand signal but leave the treats in your pouch until your dog is in the correct position. Once they lie down, then say, 'Good!' and rain praise and treats down upon them like they've just won the World Cup!

As the pair of you continue your exciting dog training journey together, you can stretch out the time between your dog lying down and you rewarding them. That way your dog will learn to lie down and chill out, safe in the knowledge that, sooner or later, you're going to pay well.

SEE, PATIENCE IS VALUABLE FOR BOTH OF _BOTH OF_ YOU TO HAVE!

LET'S TALK ABOUT YOUR DOG

Ever wondered how dogs became our most favourite companion? How you can learn to communicate perfectly with your own dog? How you can give the BESTEST strokes and how you can teach everyone else to love and appreciate dogs as much as you do?

Well, wonder no more, my brilliant friend. Read on . . .

SURVIVAL OF THE FRIENDLIEST

Take a good, long look at your dog right now. Have you ever wondered how we came to share our lives and homes so closely with wonderful dogs? How come we don't have gorgeous goats curled up on the sofa or pretty pigs patiently standing by the kitchen door waiting to be let out in the morning for a pee and a play?

Well, a big factor in why you're lucky enough to share your life with a dog comes down to the amazing ability that your dog has to be **FRIENDLY**.

Scientists believe that many thousands of years ago, even before YouTube, us humans began to settle and live in camps. Wild dogs, who are naturally shy and fearful of humans, would be in the area but the majority of them would obviously make sure they kept a safe distance from these two-legged settlers.

However, some wild dogs, the *friendlier* ones, would sneak a little closer to the campsite and sometimes be rewarded for their bravery by feeding from the waste left on the outskirts of the camp by the humans.

The friendlier dogs managed to get lots of food and nutrients from the camp without needing to hunt and risk injury trying to take down a prey animal like a deer for dinner, or waste huge amounts of energy chasing the local pizza delivery driver (joke!).

The friendlier dogs also began to hang around with each other, living off the easy food, while the more fearful ones stayed away and did the more 'wolfie' things, like howling at the moon and huffing and puffing at houses.

Over time, the friendly boy-dogs had babies with the friendly girl-dogs and guess what? Over many years, not only did those babies grow up to be even more friendly than their ancestors but their physical features changed, with their ears becoming floppier, tails becoming curlier and a wider variety of coats, colours and textures appearing.

OVER THOUSANDS OF YEARS, A POPULATION OF DOGS DEVELOPED WITH FEATURES THAT US HUMANS REALLY LIKE IN OUR PETS —

BASICALLY, THE CUTER THE BETTER !

By now, these friendly dogs were very comfortable being with humans and we adopted the very cutest-looking to be our companions.

Over time, these wild dogs evolved into domestic pet dogs that could help with hunting and act as an early burglar alarm should there be any odd noises near the settlers' campsite at night-time.

Many years passed and, due to the magic of *'the survival of the friendliest'*, hey presto, we now happily live in a world of

HUGE
Great
Danes,

tiny Chihuahuas and everything else in between!

BODY LANGUAGE

To be your dog's very best friend, and their very best trainer, I want you to be the very best Body Language Expert you can possibly be.

This may sound a little crazy, but did you know that your dog 'speaks' to you all the time using their body language?

Let me explain this another way – you can tell when your best friend is happy or sad, right? Even without them having to *say* anything!

That's what's so cool about being a best friend – you're always there to **listen** and **respond** to help your mate feel better. You can celebrate together when one of you is happy and also be there to listen and take care of each other should one of you be worried.

BE YOUR DOG'S BEST FRIEND, AND THEY'LL BE YOURS.

Have a good read of these body language signals then look out for them in your dog, as the better you are at **noticing**, **listening** and **responding** to what they 'say' with their body, the better a trainer and friend you can be!

Signs That Your Dog Is Happy And Ready To Play

 A relaxed, open mouth

A nice soft, wiggly body

 Broad tail wags, left to right

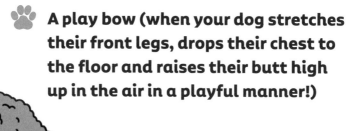

A play bow (when your dog stretches their front legs, drops their chest to the floor and raises their butt high up in the air in a playful manner!)

What Clues Can I Look Out For To See If My Dog Is Scared Or Worried?

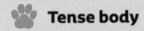 **Tense body**

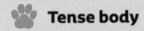 **Lowered head**

 Tail tucked between their legs

 Crouched position

 Trembling

 Slinked back ears

After A Great Day Full Of Playing And Training, How Will I Know That My Dog's Nice And Relaxed?

- Snoozing

- Soft, floppy body

- Nice long sighs as they settle down

- Snoring . . . LOUDLY!
  (If your dog is like mine!)

But hang on a minute. It's great to know about your dog's body language but how about YOURS?

Us little hairless monkey-humans communicate a lot with words but we also say a bunch with our body language, which is, of course, your dog's first language!

To ensure your dog knows you're always happy with them, make sure you:

 Don't stare hard into their eyes for ages (weirdo!)

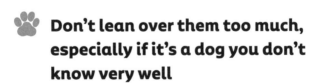 **Don't lean over them too much, especially if it's a dog you don't know very well**

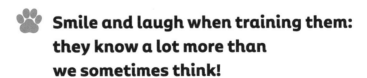 **Smile and laugh when training them: they know a lot more than we sometimes think!**

Crouch down when you encourage them to come to you

 Keep your own body nice and relaxed – don't be a stiff robot!

Rather than ambushing them, it's always best we encourage our dogs to come **to us** for a fuss . . . but hang on a minute, how do we know they **want** to be petted?

FINDING THE SWEET SPOT!

Did you know that your dog has a super-special sweet spot?

In fact, ALL dogs do!

Dogs are like us: we adore cuddles from the people we love.

So we are going to set up a

Sweet Spot Test

to find out exactly where your dog likes being stroked the most.

The more we can allow our dogs to choose to go at their own pace, the more comfortable they'll be living with us. It's much better for you to choose to go to Grandma for cuddles when you're ready, rather than her running up to you for a hug at school assembly in front of everybody when, let's be honest, the timing may not be great!

Too often, silly people (not us, of course!) call their dogs and then give them **BAD** news, such as 'Be quiet' or 'Lie there and don't beg'. That's a rubbish deal as far as the dog is concerned. Imagine your mum calling for you to come downstairs and when you eventually get to her, she says 'Do your homework!' or 'Get on with the washing up!' Rubbish news! You won't be in too much of a rush next time she calls, will you?!

THE TRICK TO BEING A DOG TRAINING GENIUS IS TO ALWAYS OFFER YOUR DOG GOOD NEWS WHEN THEY COME TO YOU.

So, when you say, 'Come!' and your dog bolts towards you all happy and enthusiastic, not only can you offer a treat or play but also a super-duper stroke right in their Special Sweet Spot.

Once you've mastered the Sweet Spot Test and you've figured out where your dog loves to be stroked, not only can you give them all that lovin' just because you're pals, but you can actually use it as one of your training rewards by generously sharing this perfect affection when your dog comes to you.

So what is a

Special Sweet Spot?

Some dogs love cuddles behind the ears (some don't) and some dogs love their butt scratched (again, some don't). My dog Pablo swoons when I scratch his chest, while my Chihuahua Nancy's legs go all wobbly when I tickle her under the chin, she loves it so much!

There's only one way to find out where YOUR dog's sweet spot is, and that's to crack on with . . .

The Sweet Spot Test.

Sit quietly on the floor in your living room and just allow your dog to hang out with you. After a few minutes of silence, hold your hand out in front of you and quietly whisper, 'Hey, buddy.' As your dog walks towards you, keep your hand still, but open and close your fingers slowly like you're scratching an elephant's forehead (what?!).

Allow your dog to lean into your 'scratchy' hand and watch them as they slowly move their body around and across your hand until they manage to hit their sweet spot . . . which is the moment you strike gold!

Give it a go!

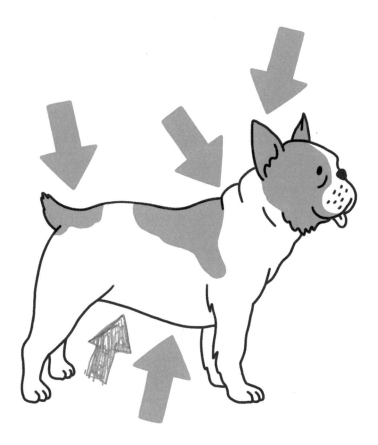

So, where's your dog's Sweet Spot?
Butt? Bely?
Chest?
Ear?
Shoulder?
Only your dog can tell you, so set up your Sweet
Spot Test, find out the magic place and swap those
perfect cuddles that only YOU can give so well for the
perfect behaviour your dog's happy to give you.

Remember, let your dog come to you for cuddles,
rather than you heading over to them.

IT'S THE PERFECT DEAL AND YOUR DOG WILL SEE YOU AS THE BEST FUSSER IN THE WORLD

THE JAR OF PAWSOME

H ere's a thing.

Dogs are AWESOME.

In fact, your dog is particularly awesome, I'd say!
Sometimes though, they may make a mistake.
They may chew your favourite book (this one,
of course!).

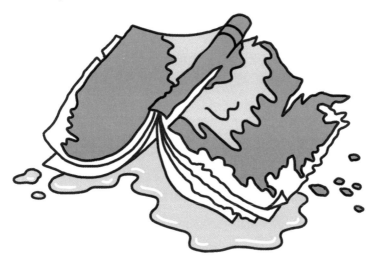

They may jump up with excitement to say, 'Hello', only to leave muddy paw prints on your favourite 'I ♥ Skool' t-shirt.

Remember though, your dog is *never naughty*, they're just doing behaviours that make perfect sense to them.

Of course, you being an **Awesome Pawsome** Dog Trainer means you're going to teach them to do *appropriate* behaviours most of the time but, let's be honest, sometimes they'll make a mistake. They're only human, after all!

When I was your age, if I saw a dog do an unwanted behaviour, I'd never shout or get annoyed, I'd simply ask myself,

I wonder why they did that?

REMEMBER,

DOGS DO BEHAVIOURS THAT 'WORK'.

BEHAVIOURS THAT GET REWARDED.

'How could I reward an *alternative* behaviour?' I'd ask myself, then get to work.

That's what I want you to do.

As I said earlier, there's no such thing as 'bad' behaviour, only behaviour you want less of!

Believe it or not, sometimes you or someone in your family will get upset with your dog if they do something you don't want them to do.

Don't let anyone get annoyed. Instead, simply reward your dog for doing *something else*, then head over to your Jar of Pawsome.

The Jar of Pawsome ? Have I not mentioned it yet?

Ah right, let me explain . . .

The next time you see an empty big jar or tub, don't throw it away – give it a good clean out and stick a label on it that says 'THE JAR OF PAWSOME'.

Now, when you and everyone in your family are in a good mood (probably a Friday night when you've done your homework and are ready to rock the weekend!), give everyone a pen and five pieces of paper. Everyone has to write down a different reason as to why your dog is so cool on each of their five pieces of paper.

It may be things such as:

They always try to make me happy.

I look forward to coming home to see their happy tail.

When I play ball in the garden with them, I forget all my worries.

Who knows what everyone will write? Just be honest and positive.

Once all the papers are written on, fold them up and pop them into the Jar of Pawsome.

Leave the Jar of Pawsome on the kitchen counter and if you ever hear anyone in your family starting to moan about the dog

(remember, it's never the dog's fault!)

then simply head over to the jar, remove the lid and offer the 'Moaner' an opportunity to pull out a piece of paper and read it aloud so everyone, *including your dog*, can hear.

Once read, ask your dog to do a nice simple behaviour for you, such as a Sit, give them a reward and then you'll all be back on track, feeling good and loving the joy that your dog brings to your family . . . and also what happiness you can bring to your dog's life.

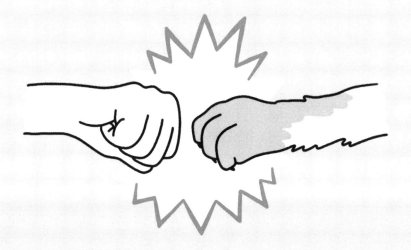

THE BEST EXERCISES TO TEACH YOUR DOG

There are some dog training exercises that we simply cannot do without!

Here, you'll find the most important exercises that will not only DEFINITELY make your and your dog's relationship better, they can actually be real life-savers!

I've included the training exercises you'll need most frequently: Recall and the Smiling Lead.

If your dog comes when you call them and walks nicely on the lead with you then, well, that's probably 99 per cent of most problems avoided!

I've also popped in the Statues exercise here, which is your dog learning to sit still for a good period of time. That's DEFINITELY going to help with Doggy Manners!

RECALL

Recall is the art of calling your dog to come to you. In fact, forget that.

Any fool can CALL their dog; the art only happens when your dog actually COMES to you!

When I was eight years old I was in the school playground at lunchtime one day with about 200 other kids when, all of a sudden, there was an eruption of screams and I saw the kids buzzing around like a swarm of bees.

I remember all this very clearly because at lunchtime there was usually never any space in our playground – every inch was always taken up by children skipping, chasing a ball or trying to steal each other's crisps! This day was different though: a huge open space opened up between the swarm of kids to reveal – to my absolute delight – a dog!

A dog?! In our playground?!

It seemed so strange and unusual.

Did you ever get that feeling when you see two things that really shouldn't go together? Like seeing a teacher on a Saturday?!

Anyway, two minutes after the dog ran into the playground, who should run in at 100mph after the dog but the freaked-out owner.

'Susie! SUSIE!' shouted the furiously flustered lady as she chased her dog.

The more she shouted, the angrier she got.

I remember thinking at the time, *Wow. If you called* **ME** *so* **ANGRILY** *like that, there's* **NO WAY** *I'd want to run to you!*

After what seemed like twenty minutes (but was probably only five) of screaming (the lady), laughing (the school kids) and running around crazily (the lady, the school kids AND the dog!), I decided to try something . . .

I knelt down quietly in the middle of the playground and pretended to be really interested in a little stone I saw on the ground.

With everyone else running around excitedly, I knew that as soon as the dog looked at me, I'd be the most interesting/peculiar/odd kid in the playground as far as Susie was concerned.

Sure enough, Susie approached me, slowed to a stop and tilted her head as she listened to me whisper, 'Look, Susie, what's this?' I slowly and carefully picked up the stone and held it gently in my hand.

As Susie came in for a closer look, I gently let her approach my hand for a stroke, as her (very) relieved owner came up behind and clipped the lead onto her dog.

'Oh Susie,' she said, 'why did you not come back when I called you?!'

'Why should she?' I said.

To myself. Not out loud. I'm not silly!

Susie's owner needed to do two things:

1) Teach Susie a really good **Recall** to save any more playground invasions.
2) Even more importantly, she had to teach Susie that her owner was **fun** to 'stay with', so there'd be no need to run off, looking for adventures elsewhere.

Now I'm going to tell you how to teach your dog a really good Recall and then we'll get into the fun activities you can play with your dog on a walk, so they'll never want to run away from you in the first place!

 In your garden or other safe space, stand with your dog and have a few tasty treats in your treat pouch. After a few moments of silence to build curiosity, shout, 'COME!' and drop a treat by your feet for your dog to find. As soon as your dog heads to eat the treat, run about ten steps away *as fast as you can*, turn and wait for your dog to raise their head from the ground once they've eaten the first treat you dropped for them . . .

As soon as their head comes up from the ground, shout, 'COME!', place another treat by your feet where you stand, then immediately run ten steps away in another direction. Turn, look at your dog and as soon as they lift their head after eating the treat . . . you guessed it, shout, 'COME!' and place another treat by your feet before again running off to your new position . . .

 Once you've done enough laps, or you're exhausted (!), call your dog one final time after they've raised their head from the previous treat. This time, as your dog runs to you, stay in the same spot, crouch down and encourage them in to you for a cuddle and a BIG handful of treats to reward them for running to you when you called 'Come!'

It's nice to finish the exercise with a big handful of treats for two reasons:

1) If you finish the session with a big prize, it will help your dog to remember the value of the game when you start your next session.

2) DOGS LOVE TREATS

THE SMILING LEAD

Unless you live in the North Pole and your dog is attached to your sled, believe me, you **DON'T** want your dog to pull you with all their strength as soon as you leave the house!

Walks are so much nicer for you and your dog once you teach them to appreciate walking WITH you, with their harness attached to a nice, *relaxed* SMILING lead. The lead is 'smiling' when it is relaxed and loose enough to hang in a curve between you and your dog.

So let's crack on and have a look at how to teach your dog ~~to not pull your arm off~~ to walk nicely with you!

I think there are three important components that we need to put together here to be successful:

1) Your dog **looking to you**
2) Your dog looking to you as you both **walk together**
3) Your dog looking to you as you both walk together **on the lead.**

As always, let's keep it nice and simple, so start somewhere safe like your garden so you don't even need the lead attached to your dog for the first stage. Let's get the behaviour right first, then we can add the lead.

With you wearing your treat pouch around your waist, drop a treat onto the ground for your dog. As soon as they've eaten it, drop another . . .

Once they've eaten the second treat, *wait* . . . this is where you need to have **super-ninja timing!**

Don't immediately throw the third treat for them – instead, wait until they look up to you in anticipation of the next goody. As soon as they look up to you, say, 'Good!' (so they know the correct behaviour is *for them to look towards you*) THEN drop the third treat for your dog to enjoy, to reward them for *looking to you*.

Looking to you is the important behaviour we want to reward here because I figure, in future, if your dog is looking at you, then they can't pull on the lead at the same time. Clever, eh?

OK, now that your dog is regularly looking back up to you after eating each treat, it's time to add our second important component: *walking together*...

Stand facing your dog, drop a treat onto the ground for them and as soon as they eat it and look back up to you, say, 'Good!' and immediately start to walk slowly in tiny little side-steps, like a crab!

I know it sounds weird but trust me, I'm a Dog Trainer!

As you side-step like a crab, keep on moving until your dog catches up with you and *pop a treat into their mouth* as the pair of you keep on shuffling along. With you still side-stepping and your dog moving along with you, as soon as they look up to you, guess what? You've got it! Say, 'Good!' and pop another treat into their mouth.

As the pair of you get more and more successful with . . .

they look up to you.

All the time saying, 'Good!' and treating your dog each time

direction, then turning and walking around in the other direction.

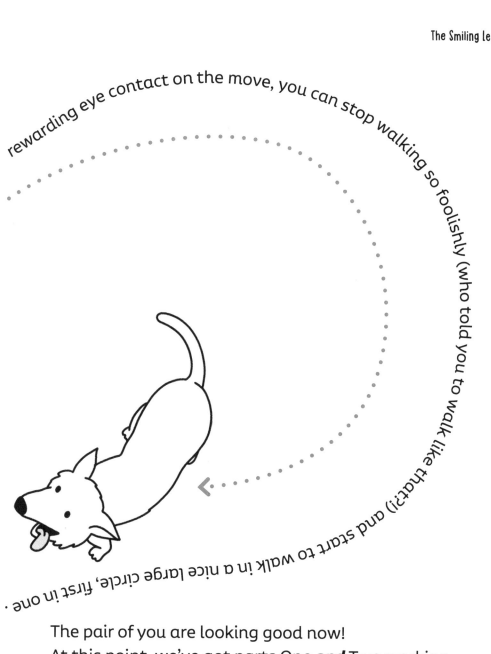

rewarding eye contact on the move, you can stop walking so foolishly (who told you to walk like that?!) and start to walk in a nice large circle, first in one . . . one in . . .

The pair of you are looking good now!

At this point, we've got parts One **and** Two working for us: your dog *looking up* to you **and** movement. Now it's time to bolt our third and final part into our training: adding the lead . . .

This bit should be easy.

Should be!

Clip the lead to your dog's harness, making sure you hold the lead by the handle so it can be nice and relaxed between your hand and your dog's harness.

As before, drop a treat then as soon as your dog eats it and looks back up to you, say, 'Good!' and pop a treat in their mouth, as the pair of you start to wander around the garden, on lead. Keep moving together and each time your dog looks up to you, reward as before.

When you start, stay away from the more *sniffy* areas of the garden such as the fence or your dad's smelly boots by the back door(!) but as you get more advanced, you can walk closer to the distractions, remembering to treat your dog and tell them how awesome they are each time they glance up to you.

Once the pair of you have mastered walking together with a relaxed lead in the garden, you can continue your practice in the park and along the pavement.

With lots of Awesome Pawsome training, you'll be able to leave longer and longer duration between treats, as your dog finds the opportunity to walk nicely with you a great reward in itself. (Don't be stingy though, we all like plenty of treats in life!)

ALWAYS STAY SAFE
AS YOU PRACTISE
TOGETHER AND
KEEP YOUR TRAINING
SESSIONS SHORT
AND SWEET —
THAT WAY YOUR DOG
WILL BE EXCITED
FOR MORE AND MORE
PRACTICE EACH DAY!

STATUE!

Let's see how many examples we can come up with for when it might be handy for our dogs to Sit stationary like a Statue for a while. Perhaps . . .

 At dinner time, to stop them jumping all over you as you dish their food into their bowl (although to be fair, I'm the same when someone opens a box of chocolates!).

 If you need your dog to stay still on the lead as you pick up their poop (what a life!).

In case a friend comes over to visit and they don't particularly like dogs (or alternatively, change your friends!).

You've already read about how to teach Sit and I know my **Awesome Pawsome** spies have reported back to me that you practise every day without fail, so let's have a look at how we can ask your dog to Sit and then act like a Statue, should you ever need a moment of stillness.

Ask your dog to Sit and when they do, softly say 'Statue', then move your right foot to the side, leaving your left foot where it is. Then count one second, bring your right foot back to join your left and if your dog has kept their butt on the floor in the Sit position, say, 'Good!' and give your dog a treat and cuddle, if they like that kinda thing! If your dog isn't much of a cuddle-bug, then use two treats and plenty of praise.

Next up, I want you to ask your dog to Sit, softly say, 'Statue', then slowly take one complete step to your right. Count two seconds and if your dog remains in their Sit position like a Statue, return to them, say, 'Good!' and be generous with the reward you give them.

The target is for you to take an additional step away from your dog after each successful attempt.

However, the real skill and demonstration of an **Awesome Pawsome** Trainer is that if your dog moves out of their Sit before you say, 'Good!', you don't see it as a failure, just information to tell you that this is the limit they're able to reach at this time.

As soon as your dog has a little wobble, and they will (unless they REALLY are a Statue!), stay cheerful and simply go back to the beginning level of Sit, followed by half a step to the right. By going back to the beginning, you're making the really clever move of building a solid foundation and illustrating to your dog that there is no rush, no pressure.

Your dog WILL be successful again, they WILL earn a fantastic treat and they WILL be happy to try their very best for you the next time you have a training session, which better be soon, or my spies will tell me!

TOGETHER YOU'VE GOT THIS!

AWESOME ACTIVITIES

What's the point of living with a dog if the pair of you can't have FUN?!

Dogs love to have fun wherever and, most importantly, with whoever they can.

If you can show your dog how to have THE best fun with YOU . . . well, you're going to be the best of pals forever.

I'm going to share with you the awesome ability *your* dog has to have the very best adventures, just by using their NOSE!

I'm also going to show you how to make the most of your walks together, how to play the best games together, and how to design fun activities so neither of you ever has the chance to get bored in each other's company!

YOUR SMELLY DOG

Your dog loves to smell.
I don't mean they love to be stinky (although they probably do!); what I mean is, they love to SNIFF.

Now, a large part of *your* brain is dedicated to *seeing* a wide range of different colours. So us humans see the world in shades of blues, yellows and reds. However, dogs can only see the world in shades of blue and yellow. Your beautiful dog doesn't see colours as well as you or I do because they have used up some of their brain space in a different way, so they can be super-duper experts in scent.

That's why, when it comes to smelling, your dog is Da BOMB!

OMG, we can't even **IMAGINE** how good your dog's sense of smell is. Yes, YOUR dog! Look at them, sitting or lying there all relaxed, you wouldn't think they're a super-hero-sniffing-machine, would you?! Proportionally speaking, the part of your dog's brain that is dedicated to analysing smells is **FORTY** time greater than yours. That brain power is needed because a dog's sense of smell is at least

times greater than ours!

WE 'SEE' THE WORLD THROUGH OUR EYES BUT A DOG PRIMARILY UNDERSTANDS WHAT'S GOING ON IN THE WORLD AROUND THEM THROUGH THEIR NOSE.

Because being able to sniff their surroundings is so important to your dog, don't be in too much of a hurry to move on the next time they feel the need to sniff a lamp post or tree. We like time to relax and read our emails. It may not seem very attractive but sometimes dogs just need a little time to kick back and read their pee-mails!

A dog's incredible sense of smell is so much more powerful than ours, which gives them an amazing ability to detect smells in places and ways that you and I can hardly imagine. I used to train dogs to detect the smell of explosives to help me find bombs, and some dogs I have worked with had the special job of searching out rare animals such as pumas and bats!

What a job!

I want you to discover and be amazed by your dog's sense of smell as much as I am by my own dogs' **super-sonic snozzers**.

Let's set up a few little searches . . .

and be prepared for your dog to
BLOW YOUR MIND!

To get started, we need to do a few of what I call 'Hides'. If your dog's already smarter than I am, you can ask them to sit while you do this. If not, it'll be best to ask your parent to hold your dog on the lead for you as you set up your search. Tell your parent you love them soooo much that you want them to be involved in your doggy search games (not only will your parents love to hear that but, let's be honest, it's so much better than tying your dog to the chair!).

With your dog watching, put five large pieces of paper on the floor and then PRETEND to place a tasty treat under a few of the pages, before finally hiding the treat under only ONE of the random sheets.

Run back to your dog and excitedly show them your empty hands as you say, 'Where is it, where's your treasure?!'

Then take your dog's lead in your hand, say, 'FIND IT!' and go out with your dog as they enthusiastically search and snuffle each piece of paper.

As soon as your dog finds and eats the treat, give them plenty of praise and cuddles – I'll be honest, I always have a little dance with my dog to celebrate their GENIUS! Go on, have a little dance, your dog will love you even more for it!

Next, do similar Hides again but perhaps use (with your parent's permission!) five mugs instead of the paper sheets, to make the search look a little different for your dog.

Next up, head out into the garden and hide the treat under one of five plant pots, or ten plant pots, or **ONE HUNDRED THOUSAND PLANT POTS!**

Why not make dinner time a million times more funky by putting your dog's dinner in a lunchbox, then hiding the lunchbox somewhere in the garden for the two of you to search and find together? (I recommend that only one of you eats it, though!)

Sometimes I like to put treats into a little box, then when I'm out walking with my dog, I'll sneakily drop the box without them seeing – once we've walked a further ten or so steps, I'll turn to my dog and say, 'Where is it, where's your treasure?' Once I've got their attention, I'll turn around, face the way we've just walked from, say 'FIND IT' and the pair of us will run back together, my dog furiously sniffing until they find the box, then BINGO! I fall to my knees, praising my dog all the time, open the lid to the box and allow my dog to enjoy their find!

Now THAT'S how to make dog walks more interesting for BOTH of you!

Dogs love to use their nose and they love people who allow them to use their nose.

The benefits us humans get from playing team games with our friends are the same benefits your dog will get from playing search games with you: fun, friendship, exciting challenges, fantastic problem-solving opportunities, confidence and, ultimately,

BOREDOM BUSTERS

Right, my friend, let's take the next few pages to come up with some Boredom Buster fun activities that don't require expensive toys or hours of training – they just need you to be generous enough to share the most important and valuable thing you ever can with your dog: TIME.

A posh word in dog training for Boredom Busters is 'Enrichment' but they both mean the same thing – 'How can we enrich the lives of our dogs?'

What do I mean by 'enrich' the lives of our dogs?

We can enrich the lives of our dogs by playing with them, being their friend, looking after them and involving them in games and activities that help them to 'exercise' all of their senses –

SMELL, <u>TASTE</u>,* TOUCH, SIGHT AND HEARING.

*My dogs have all just ganged up on me and insisted that I underline 'taste' for you. Dogs LOVE to eat!

It's really important that your Boredom Busters are pressure-free and that you always allow your dog to choose to be involved or not. Sometimes they'll be super-keen and other times they'll just want to chill, just like you or me, I guess!

No matter what age your dog is, offering Boredom Buster sessions to your canine chum is a really nice thing for you to do for them.

OK, let's get started.

Food!

I imagine that you, like me, have a favourite restaurant to eat in? But I bet if we had to eat in the **same** restaurant at the **same** table every single day without ever being allowed to eat elsewhere, it would get pretty boring!

Here's a few ideas to enrich your dog's life by creating a nice variety of different 'restaurant' settings . . .

First, with the help of an adult, I want you to raid the recycling bin. See what kit you can recycle to use as Boredom Buster containers, such as cardboard boxes, egg cartons, old newspapers or toilet roll tubes.

Take some of your dog's usual dinner or a few treats and pop the goodies inside several toilet roll tubes, scrunch up the ends so the food stays secure and then it's time to start your challenges!

First up, a nice easy challenge that will give your dog plenty of joy: simply go outside (as it will get messy!) and throw all of the stuffed toilet roll tubes out onto the garden for your dog to rip up and reveal the yummy treasure within.

A next-level challenge that will certainly last a lot longer than this feeding frenzy is if you first go out into the garden without your dog to **hide** the stuffed toilet rolls in several sneaky places before releasing your dog into the garden to use their nose and eyes to search out the goodies.

Maybe set your stopwatch and see how long it takes for your dog to find all of the treasure. If they're too quick, you're going to have to get a little sneakier with your hiding places!

Another great way to entertain your dog is to take an old newspaper, pull out each page and wrap it around an individual treat. When scrunched into a ball, throw it into a cardboard box and carry on adding more scrunched-up treat-balls. When you've run out of pages (or treats!), release your dog to rip into their treasure box in the same way I bet you do with your presents on Christmas morning!

If your dog is a bit more polite and delicate, you can make what I like to call . . .

Treat Fans

Take a page of newspaper and lay it flat on a table.

Pop a treat on the edge of the page and fold the paper over a couple of centimetres to cover the treat, then carefully turn the page over (don't let the treat drop out, or your dog will be gutted!) and repeat the process again.

Once done, you should have several treats folded carefully into what is now one long strip of newspaper.

Finally, twist the ends like a sweet wrapper to keep the tasty treats inside – you can then either give it to your dog straight away, or hide it somewhere before 'hunting' it out, together with your dog.

Remember, it's not a 'test', it's an adventure, so don't go hiding it somewhere too crazy, like buried ten metres underground or on top of a bus!

If you don't have any newspapers, or you're just feeling lazy (how DARE you!), organise the world's greatest Marmite hunt!

Pop your dog away so they can't see you, then smear a little bit of Marmite in several areas, such as a wall, the edge of garden furniture or your little sister's head (joke!) for your dog to then sniff out and lick to their heart's desire!

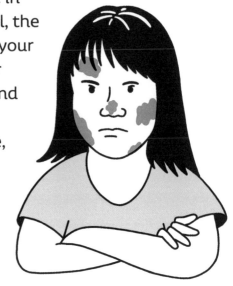

If you don't have Marmite, you could use some peanut butter or squeezy cheese.

(Hey, 'Easy Peasy Squeezy Cheesey'? Now there's an idea!)

NEVER underestimate your power to make your dog's life as awesome as possible. Boredom Busters are a really generous thing for you to do and I bet when your dog goes to bed at night after a day full of enrichment, they're dreaming about how much they love you – and of fresh new Boredom Buster adventures tomorrow!

WHATEVER BOREDOM BUSTERS YOU SET UP FOR YOUR DOG, <u>NEVER</u> FORGET TO CELEBRATE YOUR ACHIEVEMENTS TOGETHER!

HOW TO MAKE DOG WALKS THE FUNNEST THINGUS SINCE FUNNESS BEGUNUS!

Think of your best mate from school.

Now imagine going for a walk with them.

Now imagine not talking, playing or even looking at them at all for the whole duration of that walk.

It'd be a little odd, eh?

Same when you go for a walk with your dog.

Don't ignore each other.

Don't be odd!

Some people moan that their dogs don't stay with them on walks, always running off, looking for fun elsewhere. If you want your

dog to hang around you on walks, ask yourself,
Why should they? What's in it for them?

Trust me, your dog will **love** to have more fun with
YOU, so here's a few activities you can get up to
together to keep exercising not only their body but
also their brain!

Go on a 'Sniffari'

As you walk along with your dog, sneakily drop a few
items you've taken from home and had in your pocket
for a while, such as a sock (with a few treats inside it),
a face-cloth (rolled around a few cubes of cheese) or
an old wallet (delicately housing a thin slice of ham!).
Drop an item every ten steps or so and when you've
dropped all of the items,
say to your dog, 'C'mon,
buddy, let's find it!' The
pair of you can then
eagerly retrace your
steps together like
Sherlock Holmes and
Dr Watson.

Make sure you investigate every little shrub or bush until you see your dog's nose twitch at the sniff of your first find. You can whisper, 'What is it? Show me!', as the pair of you home in on your target. As soon as your dog finds the treasure, fall to your knees excitedly praising your dog, gently help them release the food, let them enjoy eating the treat, then . . . 'Let's find another!' as the pair of you go off to hunt together again . . .

Treasure Trails

Have someone trustworthy hold your dog as you walk away from them, dropping a treat every two or three steps, perhaps through some trees or around the corner. When you've walked fifty steps or so, run back to your dog (try to follow the same footsteps that you took when you were laying the trail!), take their lead and say to your best buddy, 'Where's the treasure? Show me!' Lead them to the first treat that you dropped, then follow on behind as they snuffle and search along the path, enjoying each little treat you left for them along the way. Dogs are so happy when they get to explore the world with their nose and by you creating a Treasure Trail for them, they'll get to have the **BEST** time with their **BEST** friend – YOU, of course!

Hide 'n' Seek

This one's EASY!

Simply have someone hold your dog, you give your dog a big fuss then run away and hide behind a tree. When you're out of sight, call your dog's name once, then crouch down in silence. (Oh, I forgot: make sure you arrange with the other person to let go of your dog when they hear you call your dog's name, otherwise you'll be stuck behind the tree forever!)

When I do this with my dogs, I love to try to stay as still as possible and get really excited when I hear them dashing through the leaves on the ground. If you manage to stay REALLY still, your dog will have to use their nose to find you, as they can't see super-still things very well with their eyes.

I'm not saying you stink or anything but, to your dog, you do!

Sniffaris, Treasure Trails and Hide 'n' Seeks are great activities to do with your dog and I wholeheartedly encourage you to plan such adventures for every walk you do.

ON TOP OF THAT

don't underestimate the value of a good old game together with your dog's favourite toy.

Sometimes the best games we play with our friends aren't always planned; they kinda, well, just happen!

ALWAYS BRING YOUR DOG'S FAVOURITE TOY WITH YOU ON WALKS AND SOMETIMES, JUST OUT OF THE BLUE, PULL OUT THE TOY AND HAVE A GREAT GAME OF CHASE, TUGGY OR 'SEARCH', JUST BECAUSE YOUR DOG LOVES IT!

If you randomly produce the toy and have an AMAZING game with your dog, they won't want to run away from you, because they won't want to miss out on such a great opportunity!

Let's make a list of all the essentials you should bring with you on your dog walks:

 A dog: Without your dog, a dog walk is just a walk!

 Treats: I want your dog to **ALWAYS** know you've got plenty of tasty treats with you. If your dog does any behaviour you want *more of* on your walks, such as looking to you, walking nicely on the lead, coming to you when you call or sitting when you ask, make sure you reward your dog with a treat.

Remember: **What gets treated gets repeated!**

 Toys: Dogs love activities such as chasing, grabbing and searching. YOU can provide all of that by producing your dog's favourite toy while out on walks. YOU'VE got the superpower of being able to give your dog everything they want: you're their hero!

 Poo bags: Ah, unlucky.

Going for a walk is THE best part of your dog's day. Celebrate each outing with your dog and use it as an opportunity to play, train and have fun together. It's a very special time for you both to enjoy!

THE AIM OF THE GAME

The aim of the game is to **ALWAYS HAVE FUN!** It's hard to describe that feeling you get when you're playing with your friends. You know, when you're REALLY playing. Not a care in the world, with a smile on your face and thinking of nothing other than the fun and the joy of sharing time with those you love.

Imagine having the gift of all of those amazing feelings available to you at any time of the day.

Hang on a minute, you do have such a gift . . . it's called

YOUR DOG!

Definitely, 100 per cent without a doubt, my favourite pastime is playing with my dogs.

No matter what else goes on in my life each day, I GUARANTEE I'm going to be playing with my dogs. Play is possibly the best gift I can give my dogs and it's definitely the best gift they give me, but here's the thing: the best gifts to give, and receive, are gifts that are shared with 100 per cent honesty, love and commitment.

PEOPLE GIVE THE BEST GIFTS BECAUSE THEY WANT TO, NOT BECAUSE THEY HAVE TO!

However, because we're all different, we all like different kinds of gifts. I would love to receive an Arsenal football shirt but I'd hate to receive a Tottenham Hotspur one!

So what kind of game and play style does your dog like?

Let's find out!

Sit on the floor with your dog and have a variety of toys behind your back, such as a ball on a rope, a cuddly teddy and a tuggy rope toy.

Slowly produce the toy from behind your back as you whisper to your dog, 'Oh, what's THIS?' Slowly twitch the toy along the floor in front of your dog like you're playing with a piece of string in front of a kitten.

Some dogs will watch . . . then pounce with their feet. Some dogs will grab the toy with their mouth. Some dogs will find pure ecstasy just chasing the toy along the floor as you circle it around your body.

Bring the toy to life, see what happens . . .

As I said earlier, the secret isn't really what the toy IS but what the toy DOES. You have the power to make the toy do whatever you want it to. Use your imagination. I usually find I can gain more interest and chase from my dog if I twitch the toy AWAY from them, as if the toy's a little frightened mouse looking to escape, rather than pushing the toy towards them (like a crazy mouse looking for a fight!).

Remember, there's no strict rules here, other than the most important one:

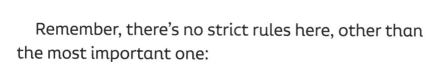

BOTH OF YOU MUST HAVE FUN!

When you're playing WITH your dog, it's good to use a toy that you can both hold on to at the same time, such as a ball on a rope or a rolled-up tea towel (with permission from the chief washer-upper, of course!).

Play is really about little competitive games. The slight difficulty with a single ball is that either YOU have it or your dog has it, so there's not much to compete over. That's why I like a ball on a rope, so your dog can hold the *ball end* to pull and you can hold the *rope end*, so you can have a gentle tug-o-war together.

Talking about tugging, the aim of the game as an Awesome Pawsome Trainer isn't to *win,* the aim of the game is to increase the amount of fun you're having together, to help your dog feel awesome about their time with you. When playing with your dog, I want you to use effort and strength *equal* to what your dog is putting into the game.

That means holding the toy first with your fingertips, not with some win-at-all-costs white-knuckle grip!

I WANT YOUR DOG TO **WIN, MANY, MANY TIMES,** SO THEY GROW TO LOVE THE GAME, THEIR CONFIDENCE INCREASES AND THEY FINISH THE PLAY SESSION LOVING THEMSELVES – **AND YOU!**

Of course, you can win a few as well but remember, no one wants to play a game where they always lose. (If they did, they'd join Tottenham Hotspur!)

If you and your dog are both holding the toy between you during play, a good trick to keep your dog engaged is to keep moving the toy, so they maintain their grip. Importantly, to keep things nice and relaxed, I want you to keep your hand movements low and slow. Keep an eye on your dog and ensure their four feet are always comfortably on the ground. Make sure their neck is never strained and don't make your hand movements front-and-back, always side-to-side, to ensure your dog stays comfortable and not too frenzied!

Be aware of your own body language when you're playing. If your body is too stiff or leaning over, your dog won't feel relaxed. When you play with your dog, *stay loosey like a goosey!*

Games with your dog may include elements of chasing, grabbing, catching, pulling, searching and finding. All perfectly acceptable behaviours when it's just a happy relaxed activity.

If, after a game, you know your dog wants to do it again, it's working. Keep it up!

IF IT'S FUN, IT'S PLAY.

EVERY DAY IS
CHRISTMAS DAY!

E veryone loves presents, right?

In fact, come to think of it, no one misbehaves when they're patiently waiting to receive a gift from a loved one, do they?

Let's see if we can combine your dog's joy of receiving presents with your very own dog-training skills to teach your dog that being polite and well behaved can make every day Christmas Day!

Let's start at the beginning: what do dogs love?

Well, they love to be with family that care for them (that better be YOU!), they love to sniff, they LOVE to eat and they love to chew.

We can turn all of those activities into 'presents' from you, by using them to **REWARD** nice, patient behaviour from your dog . . .

RIGHT, SIT UP STRAIGHT, EYES TO THE FRONT. LET'S GET TO WORK!

I want you to grab an old sports bag or similar and then pop your dog's favourite chew inside, as well as a plastic container with a few of your dog's favourite tasty treats. Sling the bag over your shoulder and head out into the garden with your dog. You are now, as far as your dog is concerned, a very young and, dare I say it, very intelligent Father Christmas!

To set the mood for your dog and to get their focus, keep all of your movements slow and relaxed. When you're slow and relaxed, your dog will be also – and being relaxed enables them to concentrate. Sometimes when people want more focus from their dog, they get louder and louder, jumping about like a lunatic, swinging toys around their head.

WRONG MOVE!

It's quiet movements and sounds from you that will build curiosity and focus from your dog.

Sit down slowly on the grass and in a whispering voice, say, 'What's this, buddy? What have I got in the bag for you today?'

With you speaking softly, your dog will learn to really tune in and listen so that they don't miss out on future treats and goodies!

As you slowly open the bag, delicately remove the container of treats like it contains the most precious jewels in the world. Gently close the bag and, with much care, open the lid of the container ever so slightly to allow your dog to sniff the magic from within!

After a few golden seconds of sniffing, wait for your dog to remove their nose from the box, then slowly take a treat out and give it to your politely waiting dog. All good things come to those that wait! If your dog becomes too impatient and starts to bump your hand with their nose or paw, simply wait until they're focused again, then slowly give them the treat to enjoy, so they can learn that waiting nicely makes good things happen!

It's important that you're not too greedy by expecting your dog to wait patiently for too long – **two or three seconds** is honestly enough. We don't want your dog to become frustrated.

Repeat this process several times, then gently pop the container back into your bag and – like the world's greatest magician – slowly produce the chew for your dog to enjoy as they sit or lie gently next to you.

IT'S GREAT WHEN YOUR DOG RELAXES AND CHILLS NEXT TO YOU. IT SHOWS YOU THEY TRUST YOU AND FEEL HAPPY IN YOUR COMPANY.

If your pupster is happy and relaxed next to you as they chew, you can gently stroke their hips and along the length of their back. Be careful not to stroke near their head, as we don't want them to worry that you might try and steal their chew from them!

If your dog's a slow chewer, you can bring a book with you to read as the pair of you chill out.

In fact, bring THIS book, it's a cracker!

When the chew is finished, give your dog a nice, slow stroke to finish off the session, safe in the knowledge that, to your dog, this time with you has probably been their favourite part of the day.

Same again tomorrow, please.

For your dog, every day can be Christmas Day!

SMARTY-PANTS
DOG FACTS

Dogs have the same senses as you and I: **taste, touch, hearing, sight and smell**, but whereas we're stronger in some senses, dogs are far superior to us in others.

Sense of Taste

Dogs aren't as fussed as us when it comes to taste. Let's be honest, they'd eat out of the kitchen bin if we let them! Here's an odd one, though: dogs are MUCH better than us at telling the difference between different types of water. Dogs can still distinguish the same flavours as us, such as bitter, sweet, salty and sour. However, when it comes to the number of taste buds for a more refined palate, us humans win. We have around 9,000 taste buds, while your dog only has about 1,700 . . . but you know what? I don't think they care!

Sense of Touch

Brace yourself, I'm about to use a posh word: **'vibrissae'.** I told you it'd be impressive, didn't I? Vibrissae are the long whiskers you'll see poking from your dog's muzzle, eyebrows and jaw.

The role of these whiskers is to 'touch' the environment around the dog's face and send messages to their brain that tell them of any sudden change in the air currents and notify them of when their mouth is close to something. THAT'S a neat trick for when your dog is trying to grab a piece of food from the floor in the dark!

Sense of Hearing

Not only are dogs better than us at hearing sounds that are further away, they can also hear a much wider range of frequencies and tones than us monkeys!

ON TOP OF THAT

with twice as many muscles in their ears as you or I, your dog's ears are mobile (I'm guessing yours aren't) AND they're able to independently move just one ear at a time (now I'm SURE you can't do that! Can you?).

Sense of Sight

When it comes to the power of sight, we tend to be the winners at spotting the finer details of what we're looking at, but dogs, with their history of hunting for a living, are better than us at spotting movements in the distance. (Handy if you need to catch a rabbit for supper!) They're also pretty good at seeing in the dark, though not as good as cats.

Us *homo sapiens* are able to see a wider variety of colours than dogs, which is why a dog has never won the snooker world championship. Although they'll never beat us at snooker, dogs do win when it comes to eyelids. Humans have two eyelids on each eye but a dog has three! The third one can swipe side-to-side to help keep the eyeball moist and remove dirt. Bit creepy that, to be honest with you!

Sense of Smell

Remember when I told you that a dog's sense of smell is up to

ONE HUNDRED THOUSAND

times better than ours? You and I may go into a bakery and smell all of the lovely bread and cakes but your dog would be able to smell all of the different, individual ingredients.

Sometimes, if you're really scared, your body will send unique body chemicals to the surface of your skin. Your dog has an amazing ability to pick up on that smell, and may well come to comfort you to try to make you feel better. Aren't dogs just the best!?

Take a look at your dog right now.

 Did you know, if she's female, she's got 320 bones in her body? If your dog's male, then he's got 321 bones. (Don't ask ME what the extra bone in a male dog's body is; that's your parent's responsibility, not mine!)

Dogs LOVE bones. Imagine if one day they realised they were actually MADE of bones?!

 Your normal body temperature is around 36–37° Celsius. Your dog's normal temperature is 38–39° Celsius.

Did you know that puppies need up to eighteen hours' sleep each day, with adult dogs needing up to a good fourteen hours of 'shut-eye'? When your dog is sleeping, it's really important that you don't disturb them, so they can confidently relax and not have to wake up in a bad mood!

 Us humans have selectively bred over 500 different breeds of dogs, resulting in a vast variety and range of sizes, body shapes and physical ability.

 A greyhound can run at amazing speeds, clocking up to forty-five miles per hour, while a pug generally likes to trot around at a more leisurely three miles per hour – as long as it's not uphill!

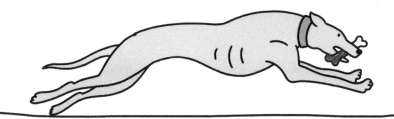

Certain breeds that enjoy swimming, like Newfoundlands and Labradors, are sometimes born with webbed feet to help them propel themselves even faster through the water. In fact, dogs are so good in the water that when the *Titanic* sank in 1912, three dogs survived!

 The heaviest breed of dog is the St Bernard, the tallest is the Great Dane, and the smallest? Well, that'd be the mighty Chihuahua.

THE BEST DOG?

THAT'S THE ONE YOU'RE WITH RIGHT NOW.

TRICK AND TREAT!

I've designed a few awesome tricks for you to enjoy teaching your dog to perform.

It's great to teach your dog lots of tricks because it's an opportunity for you to refine *your* training skills and also a wonderful chance for your dog to earn lots of great rewards!

With Trick Training, your dog may not be too used to the unusual body movements, so be careful not to overdo it.

Enjoy your Trick Training – not only is it a fab way to increase the bond and relationship with your dog, it also looks super-impressive!

HIGH FIVE!

A High Five is a really **cool** trick to teach your dog and, as always, good, positive training is going to be time well spent with your bestie!
Here's how to master the High Five . . .

1) With a tasty treat in your closed fist, hold your hand in front of your dog at about their chest height. Your dog will try several tactics to try to get the treat: they'll sniff, they'll lick and, eventually, they'll paw! As soon as your dog raises their paw to touch your fist, say, 'Good!', open your hand and let your dog enjoy their well-earned goody!

When your dog is instantly pawing at your fist as you offer it, it's time to move on to step two . . .

2) Offer your hand to your dog as before but, rather than having a treat in your fist, open your hand, palm facing upward, and keep the treat in your pouch until they paw at your hand. As soon as they do, say, 'Good!' and take a treat from your pouch and give it to your dog as you tell them what a great job they've done for you.

3) Now we need to get a little more agile . . . Rather than offering your hand with the palm facing the sky, have the palm of your hand facing your dog. It's important here that you realise that this movement will demand a lot more flexibility from your dog, so make it as easy as possible for them by offering your hand at a height you think is the most comfortable for your dog to target.

4) The final step is to add a word to the behaviour. As you offer your hand with the palm facing your dog, say in a cheery voice, 'High Five!', then as soon as your dog gives you a High Five, excitedly say, 'Good!', give them a treat from your pouch, then write to all of your aunties and uncles to tell them your dog is quite simply an

AWESOME GENIUS!

MAKE YOUR BED

Now I KNOW you're obviously the greatest human in the world at making your bed as soon as you get up, but let's try to teach your dog to be the world's greatest bed-making canine . . .

Take a nice heavy towel, lay it flat on the floor and let your dog watch you as you place a treat near the edge of the towel, between the two corners, then fold the edge of the towel over so it's covering the treat.

With your eagerly awaiting dog watching, say, 'Make your bed!' and encourage your dog to unroll the towel with their nose to reveal the treat, which they no doubt will scoff straight away! Good for them!

Next, place the treat as before near the end of the towel but this time roll the towel three times around the treat before asking your dog to 'Make your bed!'

After each successful repetition, add an extra roll of the towel so, eventually, you'll be able to roll the towel up into a long sausage shape for your dog to gently ('gently'?! Who are we kidding?!) unroll, *make their bed* and earn their tasty prize.

Now, here's the deal:

AS WITH <u>ALL</u> TRAINING, IT'S A TEAM GAME.

If your dog is struggling, help them out. It's not a boring old test.

Feel free to show them how to unroll the towel if they're confused.

(If someone comes into the room to see you rolling a towel along the floor with your nose, your dog won't be the only one who is confused!)

The towel may be slippery on the floor for them, so either teach the trick on a carpeted floor or hold the corners of the towel for your dog as they snuffle along.

I wonder if you can eventually teach your dog to Sit patiently as you roll the towel around the treat for them?

Only one way to find out!

SPIN

You know the way your PE teacher encourages you to warm up properly before playing sport, so you don't strain any muscles?

Well, I want you to do the same for your dog so they can be in tip-top sporting condition and ready for action when you pull out the **'OMG! OMG! TENNIS BALLS!'** to chase!

Before any high-energy exercise, have a little jog around with your dog so you're both ready for action, then start your Spin training . . .

Take a treat in your preferred hand and, with your dog facing you, lower the treat down towards their nose **but don't let them grab it**, or we'll be here all day!

Keep the treat at your dog's nose level and slowly move your hand a QUARTER of a circle away from you, with your dog's nose following the treat. Now, unless your dog's head is attached to their body in a VERY unusual way, as they turn to follow the treat, their head, neck, shoulders and butt shouldn't be too far away! Once your dog turns the quarter of circle away from you, say, 'Good!' and give them the treat.

The next step is to use a treat to lure your dog's nose a HALF circle away from you. Make sure you always keep the treat at your dog's nose level as you lure them around. If your dog's a big 'un, you'll need super-long arms and if your dog's a little 'un, then you'll need a nice bendy back – luckily, you're well warmed up after your jog!

Next, use a treat to lure your dog's head ALL the way around in a complete circle before giving them the treat.

The second last job is for you to start saying 'Spin!' as you lure your dog around in a circle in front of you before treating.

When you can get a perfect ten out of ten for your Spins, the FINAL step is for you to keep the treats in your pouch UNTIL you've successfully used your hand to lure your dog all the way around in front of you.

Once you can get your dog to do a Spin by luring with an empty hand, I think your dog deserves five treats as a reward from you.

I tell you what, I also think you should reward yourself with an extra chocolate biscuit (or five!) after dinner for a job well done!

WELL DONE, YOU TWO!

Oh . . . one important FINAL, FINAL job, promise!

It's important that if you, me or our dogs do an exercise going in one direction that we balance it out by repeating the exercise in the OPPOSITE direction. That way, we'll all keep healthy and well-balanced muscles. Just remember, if you say 'Spin' for going in one direction, then use the word 'Twist' when you train in the other direction.

And as a **final, final, FINAL** tip (!), if I were you, I'd use my right hand for luring clockwise and my left hand for luring anti-clockwise.

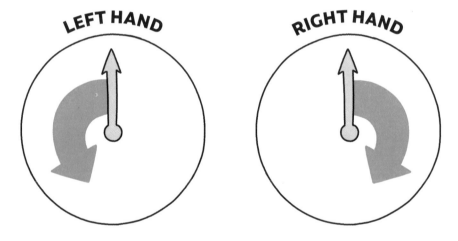

Don't tell anyone else, though – that tip is only for **Awesome Pawsome** Trainers like us!

HAND TOUCH

Right, listen up.

I want to tell you how to teach your dog a Hand Touch because not only does it look cool but . . . pull your book up closer, I don't want anyone else to see . . . it's really quite easy to teach.

Sssshhh!

A Hand Touch is when you hold the palm of your hand out flat, say 'Touch' and your dog touches the palm of your hand with their nose.

This is a great exercise to teach because if your dog loves to jump up at unsuspecting visitors, such as your granny, you can instead ask your dog to do a 'Touch' to encourage them to keep all four feet on the floor when saying 'Hi'.

If your dog is super-wiggly when the vet is trying to inspect them, then guess what trick you'll have up your sleeve (literally!) to help them out? You got it, your Hand Touch.

I love doing this nose-to-hand exercise with my dogs (with my snotty brother, not so much!).

Here's the steps I want you to take to teach this impressive exercise:

1) Place a nice big treat between the second and third finger of whichever hand is most comfortable for you to use.

2) Call your dog's name to get their attention, then place your treat-loaded hand behind your back.

3) When you're ready, bring your arm from behind your back and present the palm of your hand in front of you, about an arm's length or so from your dog's nose. Luckily, dogs are super-curious, so the lure of the treat between your fingers will entice them to move their nose towards your hand.

4) As soon as your dog's nose touches your hand, say, 'Good!' **BUT DON'T GIVE THEM THE TREAT THAT'S BETWEEN YOUR FINGERS** – instead, return that treat-loaded hand to behind your back and reward your dog with a treat *from your treat pouch*. After several successful repetitions, try a few without the lure between your fingers.

5) Once the behaviour is nice and fluent, I want you to start saying, 'Touch!' just as you present your hand for your dog to nose-bump. As soon as they do, say, 'Good!' and give them a goody from your treat pouch.

When your dog is proving to be the genius you know they are, by nose-bumping your hand each time you present it, then it's time to encourage your dog to do the behaviour for longer. Your dog will learn to actually hold their nose against your hand for a greater and greater period of time before you say, 'Good!' and pop a treat in their mouth for a job well done.

IMPORTANT:
MAKE SURE IT'S YOUR
DOG BRINGING THEIR
NOSE TO YOUR
STATIONARY HAND,
RATHER THAN YOU
MISTAKENLY BOPPING
YOUR DOG ON THE
NOSE WITH YOUR
HAND – THAT WOULD
REALLY HURT!

Let's see if we can get a little funky now and maybe start the first few steps of your own doggy dancing routine!

Rather than producing your 'touch hand' at the same level all the time, mix it up by producing it a little higher, way down low or between your legs to keep your dog engaged and to see what funky steps the pair of you can come up with together . . .

Next time there's a party at your house, turn down the lights, put the music on and hit the dance floor!

PUZZLES

When I was a kid, my brother used to love puzzles. I did too, but not the type that came in boxes. I liked the puzzle of training dogs.

Like all of the tiny little pieces of a jigsaw puzzle, each piece is small but it's vitally important to put them in the right place so that they all join together to help you achieve your bigger goal.

All the pieces of a jigsaw puzzle are important, but the corner pieces are always the ones that a clever Puzzle Master will put in place first.

When we're training a dog, what are the four important corner pieces we want in place first?

Corner One: **Trust**

Without Trust, we simply can't be **Awesome Pawsome** Trainers.

Do what you can to make sure your dog trusts you to be kind, to keep them safe, to make training fun and to set small targets that you can achieve and celebrate together.

Corner Two: **Motivation**

As an **Awesome Pawsome** Trainer, you're asking your dog to negotiate the tricky world of human beings! Sometimes it's tough for your dog. They'll try their best – so make sure that whenever they do something you like, you reward them well! If you reward your dog well for getting it 'right', they'll try even harder next time for you, to get another great reward.

Corner Three: **Achievable Targets**

It's no good trying to count to a hundred in French if you don't yet know the French word for 'one'! Likewise, you'll never learn maths well on a rollercoaster!

It's important to set very low targets in your training and to nudge your progress along – tiny step followed by the next tiny step. Set tiny targets that you can both achieve, so you and your dog will be motivated to take on the next tiny step. Also, make sure your training environment is not too distracting for you or your dog. Aim too high too soon and you'll both keep failing.

That's not Awesome, that sucks!

Corner Four: **Honesty**

Be honest with your expectations. We can't honestly ask our dog to do something if we haven't properly trained them to do so. And here's the deal: **dogs NEVER lie!** If you've trained them well to do a behaviour, when you ask for it, they'll do it. If you ask and they don't do it, no problem; it just means you haven't trained them well enough yet!

Be honest with your rewards. The important thing isn't what you think your dog SHOULD love as a reward, it's what they DO love as a reward. Some dogs love food, some love cuddles, some love toys. Take your time, find out and use what your dog LOVES to reward the behaviours YOU love.

It's a great deal!

So now you know the four important corners of any dog training jigsaw puzzle. But what about all of the other important pieces that click together to give us the final picture?

Well, we can fill in the gaps in your puzzle with fun, love, ambition, patience, skill, creativity, imagination, planning and time.

Get your four corner pieces of the training puzzle in place and enjoy clicking all of the other valuable pieces together to create a happy, confident, optimistic and enthusiastic training partner.

ENJOY YOUR NEW TRAINING ADVENTURES!

THE
CLOSING
CEREMONY

Wow!

**We've done it – we've got to the end
of a whole book!**

**I really hope you've enjoyed reading it as
much as I've enjoyed writing it for you.**

Now for the big ceremony . . .

Step forward . . .

Bow (optional!) . . .

I hereby announce that you
have achieved the grade of:

AWESOME PAWSOME DOG TRAINER!

But . . .

The journey doesn't end here; it's only just beginning.

The main duty of an Awesome Pawsome Dog Trainer is for you to **continue** to illustrate to the rest of the world that by being kind and considerate, everyone can teach their dogs to live a long and happy life with us, as **BEST FRIENDS**.

You're the future of dog training now.

You're the one that will come up with amazingly creative plans and ideas to help the dogs and owners of the future.

Be strong, be positive, be brave, and **be the Awesome Pawsome Dog Trainer your dog deserves**.

Onwards!

THIS CERTIFICATE IS PRESENTED TO

· ·

FOR COMPLETING THEIR

AWESOME PAWSOME DOG TRAINING!

DATE: ·

WORD **SEARCH**

We now know how great our dogs are at searching, but how about YOU?!

Let's see how many dog training words you can find in our Awesome Pawsome word search. Ready . . . steady . . . GO!

~~BONE~~	BOW	CHEW
~~DOWN~~	FIRST	FIVE
HAND	HIDE	HIGH
JAR	LEAD	PAWSOME
~~PLAY~~	PUPPY	PUZZLE
~~RECALL~~	SAFETY	SEEK
~~SIT~~	SMELLY	SMILING
SNIFFARI	SPIN	SPOT
~~STATUE~~	~~SWEET~~	TOUCH
TRAIL	TREASURE	TREAT
TRICKS	~~WALK~~	~~CUP~~

V D W W D H P I X I M S D P Y
V S E L I O R H H U V L C U P
E H K D O I R A F F I N S Z P
C R E C A L L S W E E T G Z U
G W U J I S D G N M O N N L P
Z J A S A R K E O U G G O E T
S R P F A Y T S C D A E L B R
J T E L K E W H G T P R B N A
C T A A A A R T N E R R O W I
Y R K T P Y S T I V C E W O L
W A L K U R T N L I B X A D E
Z S C H I E I Z I F I K J T T
T P I F G P L N M Y L L E M S
R O B T S I J P S E P H A N D
B T K E E S H R R F G L P Y S

Find the answers on page 177!

ACKNOWLEDGEMENTS

Here, most dog book authors say a cute little message of thanks to their dogs, but to be honest my dogs hardly ever read books, they're normally happy just to wait for the movie to come out.

I tell you who does read books though, the people that do all of the hard work in Publishing and those that make sure I put all my ~~order~~ words in the right ~~words~~ order. So a big thank you to Madiya Altaf, Matthew Phillips and Martin Roach.

In fact, I AM going to give a big thanks to my very special rescue Staffie called Pablo. Whenever I'm writing about dog training and I get a little stuck, I look to Pablo, who is usually snoring, chewing or annoying Nancy the Chihuahua, (sometimes all three at once!) and I ask 'How would Pablo explain this?'

Even in his sleep, Pablo is a genius and when looking at the world through his eyes, I realise we're all very special and we're all very lucky.

If you ever get stuck, look at the world through your dog's eyes.

WORD SEARCH ANSWERS

```
V  D  W  W  D  H  P  I  X  I  M  S  D  P  Y
V  S  E  L  I  O  R  H  H  U  V  L  C  U  P
E  H  K  D  O  I  R  A  F  F  I  N  S  Z  P
C  R  E  C  A  L  L  S  W  E  E  T  G  Z  U
G  W  U  J  I  S  D  G  N  M  O  N  N  L  P
Z  J  A  S  A  R  K  E  O  U  G  G  O  E  T
S  R  P  F  A  Y  T  S  C  D  A  E  L  B  R
J  T  E  L  K  E  W  H  G  T  P  R  B  N  A
C  T  A  A  A  A  R  T  N  E  R  R  O  W  I
Y  R  K  T  P  Y  S  T  I  V  C  E  W  O  L
W  A  L  K  U  R  T  N  L  I  B  X  A  D  E
Z  S  C  H  I  E  I  Z  I  F  I  K  J  T  T
T  P  I  F  G  P  L  N  M  Y  L  L  E  M  S
R  O  B  T  S  I  J  P  S  E  P  H  A  N  D
B  T  K  E  E  S  H  R  R  F  G  L  P  Y  S
```

Notes

NELLY: Blue Fun ✗✗✗

ELLIE: Blue Fun ✗✗✗✗✗

KLEO:

Even More From Steve Mann

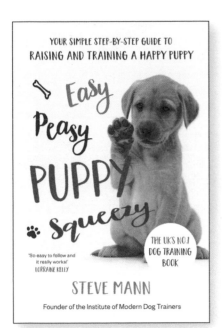